Dudley

Welsh TV Chef

First edition: September 1997
© Dudley Newbery and Y Lolfa Cyf., 1997.

Photographer: Marian Delyth
Food stylist: Kate Scale

ISBN: 0 86243 439 4

Printed and published in Wales
by Y Lolfa Cyf., Talybont, Ceredigion, SY24 5AP

e-mail ylolfa@ylolfa.com
www www.ylolfa.com

phone (01970) 832 304
fax (01970) 832 782
isdn (01970) 832 813

Dudley

Welsh TV Chef

DUDLEY NEWBERY

Published in cooperation with S4C

*This book is dedicated
to my late parents
Peggy and Bill*

*Without their help and encouragement
there's no telling what I would be doing now!*

*Thanks also to Nia, Cadi and Rhys
for being so patient.*

Contents

Vegetables and Vegetarian Meals

Dessert

Foreword

In September 1996 I published my first cookery book, in Welsh. Due to its success and popular demand it has now been translated into English.

As you can see, I started to cook when I was a very young boy under my mother's watchful eye. I loved to help – or at least that's what I thought I was doing! Dad would also cook a lot, especially Welsh Cakes. To tell you the truth, our house used to be more like a bakery in those days since there was always call for donations towards various events in the village. They were never disappointed!

It was thanks to my parents' encouragement that cookery caught my interest, and I also received support at Ysgol Rhydfelen from teachers such as Marina James and Tom Vale. I'm also indebted to Dick Connop who gave me my first job as trainee chef after leaving college. It was his training and support that made me carry on.

Somehow, it felt perfectly natural for me to start introducing cookery to other people. I'd had years of experience of working in various fields connected with cookery since leaving college, and I loved meeting people, exchanging ideas, discussing recipes, etc. First of all came the radio series 'Pryd o Dafod' and then I was offered a series of cookery slots on 'Heno'. Since then I have presented three cookery series of my own and a fourth will be screened in January 1998. The series is naturally called 'Dudley', and shows what variety of recipes you can prepare with the best Welsh ingredients.

The climate and terrain in Wales allows it to produce lamb and beef very naturally. Welsh lamb and Welsh beef is among the finest in the world, and in this book you will have the chance to prepare Welsh food in original and exciting dishes.

I think that the only advice I can give you is the same as I give on my television shows, which is to enjoy your cooking and don't be afraid to adapt recipes to suit your own tastes. Hopefully this is a collection of tasty, fuss-free recipes - you won't need to spend hours in the kitchen preparing them, I promise! But I hope, more than anything, that these recipes will inspire you to create your own unique, tasty meals; remember that Dudley's advice is GO FOR IT!

DUDLEY NEWBERY

Electric / Gas Oven Temperatures

Remember that you will need to preheat the oven for 10 - 15 minutes (depending on your oven) before starting to cook some dishes.

	Gas	*Degrees C*	*Degrees F*
Cool	¼	110	225
	½	120	250
Fairly Cool	1	140	275
	2	150	300
Moderate	3	160	325
	4	180	350
Warm	5	190	375
	6	200	400
Hot	7	220	425
	8	230	450
Very Hot	9	240	475

Measuring Units

The tables below are only a rough guide. Remember not to combine measurements – choose one system and keep to it. Unless stated otherwise, level spoonsful should be used in the recipes. A tablespoon is 15 ml and a teaspoon is 5 ml, with one measure of alcohol being equal to 25 ml. The eggs used are usually size 2.

Weight		Volume		Measurements	
½ ounce	15 grams	2 fluid ounces	55 ml	¼"	5mm
¾	20	3	75	½	1cm
1	25	5 (¼ pint)	150	¾	2
1½	40	½ pint	275	1	2.5
2	50	¾	425	1¼	3
2½	65	1	570	1½	4
3	75	1¼	725	1¾	4.5
4	110	1¾	1 litre	2	5
4½	125	2	1.2	2½	6
5	150	2½	1.5	3	7.5
6	175	4	2.25	3½	9
7	200			4	10
8	225			5	13
9	250			5¼	13.5
10	275			6	15
12	350			6½	16
1 pound	450			7	18
1½	700			7½	19
2	900			8	20
3	1.35 kg			9	23

Basic Recipes

Egg Pasta

1 lb/450 g strong plain flour
1 tsp salt
4 large eggs
1 tsp olive oil

1. Sift the flour and salt into a mixing bowl.
2. Make a well in the centre, break the eggs into it and add the olive oil.
3. Mix together thoroughly.
4. Knead the dough for 10-15 minutes until smooth and elastic.
5. Leave for 1 hour or store overnight in the fridge.

Egg pasta may be used in a variety of recipes such as spaghetti, lasagne, cannelloni and tagliatelle. Various sauces may be used to accompany it.

Shortcrust Pastry

1. Sieve the flour and salt into a bowl.

2. Rub lard and butter into flour with fingertips until the mixture resembles breadcrumbs.

3. Make a well in the centre and add the water, a little at a time. Stir with a knife until mixture forms a ball.

4. Knead the ball lightly, ensuring that the pastry sticks together. Remember not to knead the pastry for too long or it will be difficult to roll and might become hard after baking.

8 oz/225 g plain flour
pinch of salt
2 oz/50 g lard
2 oz/50 g butter
2/3 tbsp cold water

This pastry is suitable for use in a fruit tart or a savoury dish such as a pasty.

Sweet Shortcrust Pastry

9 oz/250 g plain flour
4 oz/110 g butter
4 oz/110 g icing sugar
pinch of salt
2 eggs at room temperature

1. Place the butter, icing sugar and salt in a bowl and blend with your hands or a wooden spoon until the mixture softens and becomes creamy.

2. Add the eggs and mix again.

3. Gradually add flour to the mixture. Mix well to combine ingredients. Knead pastry lightly with the palm of your hand. When even, roll pastry into a ball and flatten slightly before sealing in clingfilm or a polythene bag.

4. Leave pastry to rest in the fridge for a few hours: this will make it easier to handle.

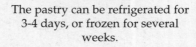

The pastry can be refrigerated for 3-4 days, or frozen for several weeks.

Irish Soda Bread

1. Mix dry ingredients with the milk.

2. Shape dough into a round, then divide into triangles.

3. Bake on a hot bakestone, or in the oven for 30-45 minutes: gas mark 7, 425°F/220°C.

1 lb/450 g plain flour (or a mix of plain & brown flour)

1½ tsp salt

1 tsp bicarbonate of soda

1 tsp cream of tartar

1 pt/570 ml sour milk or buttermilk

To make Sweet Soda Bread add 2 oz/25 g sugar, 1 egg and 2 oz/25 g sultanas.

Stuffing

3 oz/75 g butter

1 onion, finely chopped

8 oz/225 g breadcrumbs

4 tbsp parsley, finely chopped

2 tbsp thyme

salt & pepper

1. Melt butter in a pan and cook onion gently.

2. Add remaining ingredients and stir well.

3. Either place stuffing in a greased baking tin and bake in the oven for 20 minutes: gas mark 4, 350°F/ 180°C. Or shape into balls and roll in wholemeal flour; place on a baking sheet and bake for 10 minutes: gas mark 4, 350°F/ 180°C.

Cranberry Sauce

1. Rinse cranberries.

2. Place all the ingredients in a pan and cook gently for 15 minutes until cranberries begin to soften.

3. Reduce sauce until slightly thickened and pour into a jar.

4. Leave to cool.

1 lb/450 g fresh cranberries
6 fl oz/175 ml water
3 tbsp caster sugar
5 fl oz/150 ml port

You could add strips of orange rind to the sauce before cooking it. Orange complements the cranberry flavour extremely well.

Store sauce in fridge.

Brandy Sauce

1 pt/570 ml milk
2½ tbsp sugar
1 dsp cornflour
2 tbsp water
whipped double cream
3-4 tbsp brandy

1. Pour milk into pan and add sugar.

2. Bring to the boil, then pour into a bowl.

3. Mix cornflour with water.

4. Add cornflour paste gradually to milk, stirring thoroughly.

5. Add brandy to milk mixture before pouring back into pan and heating gently. Remember to keep the heat low or the sauce might stick to the bottom of the pan and burn.

Barbecue Marinade

1. Soak suitable pieces of meat in your choice of marinade overnight.

2. Light barbecue and allow it to heat adequately, then cook meat. Remember that sugar in the honey will cause the sauce to burn on the barbecue, so keep a close eye on the food.

3. Serve with salad.

Marinade 1:

1 tbsp peanut butter

2 tbsp sesame oil

tabasco sauce or chilli oil (to taste: these are very hot, so take care)

1 tbsp honey

Marinade 2:

2 tbsp chilli pickle/relish

2 tbsp tomato sauce

juice of 1 lemon

4 tbsp oil

Marinade 3 – for lamb:

1 tsp rosemary

1 tbsp honey

1 tbsp wholegrain mustard

1 tbsp soy sauce

5 tbsp oil

You could use mushrooms, sweet peppers or any vegetables of your choice instead of meat if you are catering for vegetarians.

Barbecued baby sweetcorn are very tasty. Wrap them in foil with a little oil, salt, pepper and a spoonful of honey.

Snacks

Rösti Potatoes

1½ lbs/700 g potatoes
½ onion, finely chopped
3 bacon rashers
1 oz/25 g butter
2 tbsp parsley, chopped
salt & pepper
olive oil for frying

1. Boil potatoes in their skins, then allow to cool before peeling.

2. Grate potatoes into a bowl and add the onion.

3. Grill bacon, then cut into strips and add to potatoes and onions.

4. Dice butter finely and add, together with the parsley, to other ingredients. Season and mix well.

5. Heat frying pan, adding a little olive oil. Add potato mixture, pressing firmly into base of pan.

6. Cook over a medium heat for 15 minutes.

7. Place a plate (face down) on top of frying pan then invert potatoes onto plate.

8. Carefully slide potatoes off plate and back into pan. Cook for a further 10-15 minutes.

Golden Cheese & Onion Sandwich

1. Place cheese and onion on one slice of bread, then cover with the other slice. Place sandwich in a shallow bowl.

2. Beat the egg and add Cayenne pepper and seasoning.

3. Pour egg over sandwich and leave to stand for about half a minute before turning sandwich over. Then leave to stand for a further half a minute.

4. Melt a knob of butter in a frying pan, ensuring it doesn't burn. Fry sandwich until golden on both sides.

2 slices bread & butter
2 oz/50 g mature Cheddar cheese
1 tbsp onion, finely chopped
1 egg
pinch of Cayenne pepper
salt & pepper
unsalted butter for cooking

You could experiment with different fillings – such as ham and tomato, or sliced sausage with slivers of pineapple.

Take care when turning the sandwich in the pan.

Welsh Rarebit

1 oz/25 g butter

½ oz/15 g plain flour

¼ pt/150 ml milk

4 oz/110 g grated Cheddar cheese

1 egg yolk

4 tbsp beer

1 tsp Worcestershire sauce

½ tsp hot mustard

pinch of Cayenne pepper

salt & pepper

1. Melt butter in a pan. Add flour and stir well over a medium heat for 2 minutes.

2. Continue to stir while adding the milk, a little at a time.

3. Add cheese and cook over a low heat until cheese has melted.

4. Add egg yolk and stir well.

5. Add the beer and the remaining ingredients; stir well. Allow to cool.

6. Butter some toast. Thickly spread with cheese mixture.

7. Grill for 5-10 minutes until golden and bubbling.

Samosas

4 tbsp vegetable oil

1 onion, finely chopped

1 tbsp grated fresh ginger

1 green chilli de-seeded and finely chopped

6 oz/175 g peas (fresh or frozen)

1 lb 10 oz/750 g boiled potatoes

2 tbsp lemon juice

1 tsp garam masala

¼ tsp Cayenne pepper

1 tsp coriander

1 tsp crushed cumin seeds

1½ tsp salt

2 tsp fresh coriander leaves, finely chopped

For the dough:
½ lb/225 g plain flour

4 tbsp oil

4 tbsp water

½ tbsp salt

oil for frying the samosas

1. Heat the oil in a pan and fry the onion, ginger and chilli until soft.

2. Cook the peas for approximately 4 minutes.

3. Cut the potatoes into small pieces before adding them – together with the peas – to the ingredients in the frying pan. Add the lemon juice, herbs and seasonings, and mix together.

4. Cook for 15-20 minutes and leave to cool.

5. For the dough, sieve the flour into a bowl and add the water, oil and salt, mixing them together well with a spoon.

6. Leave the dough to stand in a polythene bag for half an hour before using it.

7. Cut the dough into 8 small pieces. Place in a bowl covered with a damp cloth and take the dough pieces out one at a time, shaping each one into a little ball.

8. Roll each ball into a 7"/18 cm circle and cut in half.

9. Fold each half once to create a cone shape and stick the sides of the dough together.

10. Spoon a little of the vegetable mixture into each cone and press together top of the dough to form a neat parcel.

11. Deep-fry the parcel for a few minutes until the dough begins to brown.

Corned Beef & Sweet Potato Rissoles

1. In a large bowl, chop the corned beef.

2. Add remaining ingredients and mix well with two spoons or, if you prefer, with your hands.

3. Shape mixture into walnut-sized balls.

4. Roll rissoles in coating ingredients, flour first then beaten egg.

5. Finally coat well with breadcrumbs.

6. Deep-fry rissoles for 5-7 minutes; use a chip pan/deep fat fryer if possible.

Serves 4-5

Rissoles:

1 large tin corned beef

1 lb/450 g sweet potatoes, cooked and mashed

½ onion, finely chopped

1 small leek, finely chopped

2 cloves garlic, crushed/finely chopped

½ chilli, finely chopped

1 tbsp pine kernels

2 tsp ground cumin

2 tbsp coriander leaves, finely chopped

1 tsp fresh ginger, grated

salt & pepper

Coating:

1 cup plain flour

2 eggs, beaten

½ loaf, breadcrumbs

oil for frying

Stir-fry: Meal For One

1 tbsp oil

½ oz/15 g butter

1 rasher bacon, chopped

1 clove garlic, finely chopped

1 oz/25 g fresh (or canned) baby sweetcorn

¼ sweet red pepper, sliced

1 stick celery, sliced

2 oz/50 g prawns

2 oz/50 g chicken pieces

2 oz/50 g ham pieces

salt & pepper to taste

1 tbsp soy sauce

1 tbsp tomato purée

4 oz/110 g boiled rice

Keep the ingredients moving in the pan to prevent sticking.

Don't overcook the ingredients.

Use a wok if possible, but a frying pan or saucepan will do.

1. Melt butter with oil in a wok or pan.

2. Add bacon and garlic and fry until starting to brown.

3. Add sweetcorn, red pepper and celery. Cook for a further minute.

4. Add prawns, chicken and ham and stir well.

5. Add seasoning and soy sauce to taste. Take care with the soy sauce – different types vary in strength.

6. Add tomato purée and boiled rice.

7. Keep stirring thoroughly until piping hot and cooked through.

Potatoes in a Hot Tomato Sauce

1. Heat oil in a deep frying pan or saucepan and fry onion with Cayenne pepper and cumin seeds.

2. Add tomato juice, water and potatoes. Stir well.

3. Simmer for 20-30 minutes, or until potatoes are cooked.

Serves 4

olive oil for frying
½ onion, finely chopped
¼ tsp Cayenne pepper
½ tsp cumin seeds
½ pt/275 ml tomato juice
½ pt/275 ml water
2 lbs/900 g new potatoes, scrubbed

Soups &
Starters

Mushroom Soup

4 oz/110 g butter

1 onion, chopped

3 cloves crushed garlic (or to taste)

1"/2.5 cm root ginger, grated (or ground ginger to taste)

2 lbs/900 g mushrooms

salt & pepper

½ cup plain flour

2 pt/1.2 l chicken stock or vegetable stock (use 2 stock cubes)

½ pt/275 ml double cream

chopped parsley to garnish

1. Melt the butter in a pan.

2. Add onion, garlic and ginger. Cook until softened before adding mushrooms. Stir well.

3. Season to taste.

4. Add flour. Stir well to coat mushrooms.

5. Add stock a little at a time; stir well between additions. Using hot stock will make the blending process easier.

6. Simmer gently for about 20 minutes.

7. Add cream and parsley just before serving.

Generally, dried herbs and spices taste stronger than fresh, so add the ginger gradually, tasting the soup between additions.

Don't brown the garlic. This will give the soup a burnt taste.

Mixed Vegetable Soup

12 oz/350 g mixed vegetables
(onions, leeks, carrots, cabbage,
celery and turnips)

2 oz/50 g butter

1½ pt/850 ml stock

1 oz/25 g peas

1 oz/25 g French beans

salt & pepper

1. Peel and prepare the mixed vegetables, then cut into even sized (½"/1cm) cubes – remember, the larger the cubes, the longer it will take the vegetables to cook.

2. Melt the butter in a large saucepan and add the prepared vegetables (not the peas or beans). Cook over a low heat to soften the vegetables. Cover pan to prevent steam from escaping.

3. Add hot stock – use a stock cube if you don't have any fresh stock. Add salt and pepper and cook for about 30 minutes.

4. Add peas and beans. Simmer gently until vegetables are cooked.

5. Skim fat from surface. Adjust seasoning to taste.

Celery, Leek and Potato Soup

1. Melt butter in a large pan and fry onion over a low heat until softened.

2. Add celery and potatoes and stir well.

3. Add stock and bring to the boil.

4. Add salt and pepper to taste.

5. Cover and cook over a high heat for 45 minutes, or until celery and potatoes are soft.

6. Add leek and simmer for a further 10 minutes.

7. Remove from heat and add half the cream and parsley.

8. Serve in warmed soup bowls and decorate with remaining cream and parsley.

9. Serve with brown bread rolls or soda bread.

3 oz/75 g butter

1 onion, finely chopped

4 sticks celery, finely chopped

4 large potatoes, peeled and cubed

2 pt/1.2 l chicken stock or vegetable stock

salt & pepper

1 leek, finely chopped

3 fl oz/75 ml double cream

2 tbsp fresh parsley, finely chopped

Pâté

5 oz/150 g butter

1 onion, chopped

2 cloves garlic, chopped

1 lb/450 g chicken livers

1 tbsp parsley, finely chopped

2 bay leaves

a good measure (2 tbsp/30 ml)
brandy or sherry

2 fl oz/55 ml cream

salt & pepper

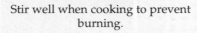

Stir well when cooking to prevent burning.

Season well. This will improve the flavour when cooking.

1. Melt 2 oz/50 g of the butter in a frying pan. Add onion and garlic and cook until soft.

2. Add livers and fry gently. Add parsley, bay leaves and the brandy/sherry. Flame quickly, but take care!

3. Add cream and stir well. Leave to cool slightly.

4. Place mixture in liquidizer and blend for 2-3 minutes.

5. Melt 3 oz/75 g butter, then add to mixture in liquidizer. Blend for a further few seconds. The additional butter will help the pâté to set.

6. Pour mixture into a small bowl and cover with more melted butter. The butter will help to keep the pâté fresh and will prevent the surface from discolouring and drying out.

7. Place in the fridge until set.

8. Serve with crusty bread or toast.

Smoked Mackerel Pâté

8 oz/225 g smoked mackerel fillets

4 oz/110 g fromage frais

4 oz/110 g cottage cheese

1 tsp horseradish, grated

1 tbsp lemon juice

salt & pepper

paprika, to taste

1 tbsp fresh parsley, finely chopped

1 tbsp stale wholemeal breadcrumbs

lime slices and radicchio leaves to garnish

1. Place mackerel, fromage frais, cottage cheese, horseradish and lemon juice in a food processor and blend until smooth.

2. Add salt, pepper, paprika, parsley and breadcrumbs and mix well.

3. Transfer to a bowl and chill for 30 minutes.

4. Garnish pâté with lime and radicchio. Serve with wholemeal bread toast triangles.

Yoghurt Dip with Crudités

1. Mix yoghurt, chives and parsley. Add salt and cayenne pepper.

2. Pour dip into a small serving dish. Sprinkle over a little paprika.

3. Arrange vegetables on a serving platter. Place dip bowl in the centre of the platter. Serve.

Dip:

8 oz/225 g strained Greek yoghurt

1 tbsp chives, finely chopped

1 tbsp parsley, finely chopped

salt & cayenne pepper

paprika, to garnish

Crudités:

4 oz/110 g button mushrooms

2 carrots, cut into strips

1 celery, cut into strips

2½"/6 cm cucumber, cut into strips

½ red pepper, cut into strips

¼ green pepper, cut into strips

8 spring onions, trimmed

Mushrooms in a Garlic Sauce

3 oz/75 g butter

2 onions, finely chopped

5 cloves garlic, finely chopped

2 lbs/900 g mushrooms, halved

2 tbsp parsley, finely chopped

4 fl oz/110 ml double cream

1. Melt butter in a pan and fry onions and garlic until softened.

2. Add mushrooms.

3. Cover pan and cook over a medium heat for 15 minutes.

4. Add parsley and cream; stir well. Cook for a further 5 minutes before serving.

Pickled Salmon

1½ lb/700 g salmon tails

For the pickle:
1 tbsp salt
1 tbsp granulated sugar
1 tsp crushed black peppercorns
1 tsp brandy (optional)
1 tsp fresh dill

For the sauce:
2 tbsp French mustard
1 tbsp granulated sugar
1 large egg yolk
7 tbsp olive oil
2 tbsp white wine vinegar
salt & pepper to taste

1. Fillet the fish tails.

2. Mix all the pickling ingredients together in a bowl and spread a quarter of the mixture over the base of a flat dish.

3. Place the first piece of salmon (skin down) in the marinade and spread half of the remaining pickle over the top of the salmon.

4. Place the other fillet of salmon (flesh down) on top of the first and cover with the remaining pickle.

5. Cover the dish with foil; use weights to press the salmon down. Refrigerate for anything up to 5 days (but not less than 12 hours), turning the salmon once a day.

6. For the sauce, beat the egg yolk, the mustard and sugar together until smooth. Then gradually add the oil and vinegar, mixing together well after each addition. Season to taste.

7. Slice the fish thinly and serve with the sauce.

Melon Castle with Bayonne Ham

━━━━━━

1. For the dressing, boil the vinegar, sugar and half the chillies in a pan and let them reduce to half their original consistency. Add a few more chillies if desired. Set the sauce aside to cool. (This may be kept in a Kilner jar.)

2. Cut the melon in half and remove the seeds.

3. Take one of the melon halves and, starting from the middle (the widest part) and working your way towards the end, cut into 4 round slices. Then cut each of these 4 slices diametrically in half. You should now have 8 semicircular segments of melon.

4. Place the strawberries in a bowl and add a little black pepper and a little of the chilli dressing – about 1-2 tablespoons.

5. To construct the melon castle, first place the 2 smallest semicircular segments side by side, flesh uppermost, on a plate, to form a circle. Leave a gap of ½"/1 cm in between. Place another 2 semicircular segments of melon on top of the first 2 so as to bridge the ½"/1 cm gap between them. Construct the melon castle or bowl by repeating this process until you have used all 8 semicircular segments.

6. Place the strawberries in the melon bowl thus constructed and take 3 slices of ham and leave to trail over the sides.

7. Repeat with the second half of the melon.

8. To decorate, place sprigs of chervil in between the pieces of ham.

Serves 2

1 red chilli, finely chopped
1 green chilli, finely chopped
3 oz/75 ml white wine vinegar
3 fl oz/75 g sugar
1 Charentais or Ogen melon
4 strawberries, quartered
black pepper
6 thin slices Bayonne or Parma ham

chervil to garnish

Melon Crown

1 Galia melon
¼ apple, finely chopped
½ stick of celery, finely chopped
2 oz/50 g prawns

For the sauce:

2 tbsp mayonnaise
1 dsp tomato ketchup
1 tsp Worcester sauce
salt & pepper to taste

Lemon slices and finely chopped
parsley to garnish

If you can't get fresh prawns, frozen ones will do, but remember that they tend to have a high water content.

To prevent the apples from discolouring, coat them in lemon juice and immerse in water.

When preparing the sauce, remember that you can adjust the ingredients to suit your taste; for a special occasion, you could add brandy and some cream.

1. Cut the melon into a crown shape. Remove the seeds.

2. Remove a little of the flesh also to make room for the filling. Don't throw it away – keep it to use in a fresh fruit salad.

3. Place the apple and celery in the melon in layers and add the prawns on the top.

4. Add the sauce: be careful not to use too much.

5. Decorate the melon with the lemon and parsley before serving.

6. This recipe may be prepared in advance, but don't add the sauce until the last minute.

Mushrooms and Onions in Sherry

2 oz/50 g butter
1 onion, chopped
1 lb/450 g mushrooms
2 tbsp plain flour
4 tbsp parsley, finely chopped
6 fl oz/175 ml vegetable stock
2 fl oz/55 ml sherry or brandy
salt & pepper

1. Melt butter in a pan and fry onion until soft.

2. Add mushrooms and cook until almost softened.

3. Add flour, stir well.

4. Add stock and stir well until sauce thickens. Add the sherry/brandy. Cook over a high heat for a further 5 minutes. Season to taste and stir in parsley.

Fish & Seafood

Salmon in an Orange and Tarragon Sauce

6-8 oz/175-225 g salmon,
per person

butter

sprig of fresh tarragon, per person

½ tbsp orange rind, finely chopped

salt & pepper

½ tbsp dry white wine

Sauce:

3-4 tbsp orange vinegar

2 tsp sugar

rind of 1 orange, cut into strips

4 tsp tarragon, finely chopped

½ oz/15 g butter

1. Ensure that there are no bones in the salmon.

2. Cut two pieces of foil which are large enough to cover the fish. Place a knob of butter and a sprig of tarragon on one of the foil squares, and place the fish on top of it.

3. Sprinkle over the fish some orange rind, salt, pepper, wine and a pinch of chopped tarragon.

4. Cover fish with the other foil square. Seal the parcel securely.

5. Place parcel in oven and cook for 10 minutes: gas mark 7, 425°F/220°C.

6. To prepare sauce, heat orange vinegar in a pan over a medium heat. Then add sugar and stir.

7. Allow sugar to dissolve, add orange rind, tarragon and butter.

8. Stir well. Remove from heat when butter has melted.

9. Serve fish with sauce poured over.

Marinated Hake

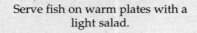

Serves 4

4 pieces hake
1 bayleaf
juice of 1 lemon
1 tbsp olive oil
2 cloves garlic, finely chopped
2 tsp ground coriander
salt & pepper

1. Shred bayleaf and place in a shallow bowl which is large enough to hold the fish comfortably. Add the lemon juice, oil, garlic, coriander and seasoning and mix well.

2. Place fish in marinade, skin side up. Leave to stand for 1½-2 hours, turning two or three times.

3. Grill the fish under medium heat for 5-10 minutes, basting with remaining marinade.

Serve fish on warm plates with a light salad.

Haddock Goujons

1. Slice the haddock into 2"/5 cm strips.

2. Pour beaten egg into a shallow dish.

3. Season flour and place on a plate.

4. Coat fish strips in flour before dipping in the egg, then roll in breadcrumbs.

5. Refrigerate the coated fish while you prepare the sauce.

6. In a medium-sized pan, gently cook onion in butter until softened.

7. Add the mushrooms and flour and cook for a further 2 minutes.

8. Remove pan from heat, gradually add milk, stirring well. Return pan to a medium heat and cook sauce for 10 minutes. Stir well until sauce thickens. Season well and add cream. Keep sauce warm.

9. Fry goujons in hot oil until golden brown. Serve with warm sauce and garnish with lemon wedges and parsley.

Serves 2

1 lb/450 g fresh haddock, skin and bones removed

1 egg, beaten

3 tbsp flour

salt & pepper

fresh white breadcrumbs

oil for frying

Sauce:

½ medium onion, finely chopped

2 oz/50 g butter

4 oz/110 g white mushrooms, sliced

1 tbsp plain flour

2 fl oz/55 ml warm milk

salt & pepper

8 fl oz/225 ml double cream

lemon wedges & parsley to garnish

Ask your fishmonger to remove skin and bones from fish.

Baked Cod and Potatoes

Serves 4

6 large potatoes
1 lb/450 g cod, cubed
seasoned flour for coating
½ lb/225 g mushrooms, sliced
1 bunch spring onions, chopped
oil for frying

Sauce:
2 oz/50 g butter
2 tbsp flour
8 fl oz/225 ml milk
8 oz/225 g hard cheese, grated
breadcrumbs

1. Scrub the potatoes and cook in a microwave oven on a high setting for 5 minutes each. Then slice thinly lengthways.

2. Roll cod in seasoned flour.

3. Fry mushrooms and spring onions in oil.

4. To prepare sauce, melt butter in a pan, add flour and stir well.

5. Gradually add milk, stirring well. Then add cheese, setting aside a little for garnishing.

6. In an ovenproof dish approximately 8" x 5"/20 cm x 13 cm deep, arrange a layer of potatoes, then a layer of fish, then a layer of mushrooms, seasoning well between each layer. Repeat layers ending with a layer of potatoes.

7. Pour over cheese sauce and sprinkle dish with remaining cheese and breadcrumbs.

8. Bake in oven for ¾-1 hour: gas mark 4, 350°F/180°C.

Hake Provençale

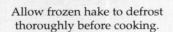
1. Heat oil in a frying pan, then add butter.

2. When the pan is hot, add onion and garlic and cook until softened.

3. Add orange rind.

4. Stir well and gradually add tomatoes, wine and tomato purée. Stir well before adding basil.

5. Finally add fish to the pan and cook for 6-8 minutes. Serve garnished with fresh basil leaves.

Seabass in a Mead Sauce

½ oz/15 g sugar

1 tbsp white wine vinegar

5 fl oz/150 ml Welsh mead

olive oil for frying

14 oz/400 g sea bass

salt & pepper

2 oz/50 g butter

mixed solverino vegetables
(tomato, cucumber and carrots –
blanch the carrots beforehand)

fresh chervil

Cook fish quickly in hot oil to seal in juices.

Don't allow the mead to boil when adding the butter or the sauce will separate. If you don't want to use butter, you could use a little cornflour blended with cold water to thicken the sauce.

Parsley or tarragon can be used instead of chervil.

1. Preheat oven to gas mark 7, 425°F/220°C.

2. In a heavy based pan, cook sugar, vinegar and mead until they become caramelized.

3. Heat oil in a frying pan, add fish and season. Brown lightly on both sides. Then place on a baking sheet in the oven for 5 minutes while preparing the sauce.

4. Gradually add butter to caramel and reduce sauce slightly over a medium heat. Beat well with a whisk.

5. Add mixed vegetables, stir and heat through. Finally add chervil.

6. Remove fish from oven and serve with sauce.

Fried Mackerel

---

1. Heat the oil in a frying pan and add the butter.

2. Add mackerel and fry for 4 minutes on each side. Remember to make sure that it doesn't stick and burn.

3. Add the lime juice and rind; turn the fish in the juice.

4. Add the coriander and a little brandy or wine.

5. Keep moving the fish in the pan and cook for a further minute or two before serving.

---

1 tsp olive oil

1 oz/25 g butter

8-10 oz/225-275 g fresh mackerel per person

grated rind of a lime

juice of half a lime

2 tbsp fresh coriander leaves, finely chopped

good measure of brandy or white wine

When choosing the fish, make sure it has a good coating of slime and that it isn't too soft.

Make sure that the eyes are black and clear.

Whilst frying, keep the fish moving or it will stick to the pan.

You could vary the ingredients to suit any type of fish – what about skate or sole with butter and lemon juice?

If you don't have fresh coriander, you could use dried coriander, but add it sparingly.

King Prawns

Serves 2

2 oz/50 g butter
3 cloves garlic, crushed
4 shallots, finely chopped
2"/5 cm ginger, grated
6 king prawns
5 fl oz/150 ml medium sherry
2 tbsp fresh parsley, chopped
salt & pepper

1. Melt butter in a large frying pan and add the garlic, shallots and ginger.

2. Cook over a medium heat for 2 minutes, or until mixture is soft and golden brown.

3. Add king prawns and turn in the garlic for a minute.

4. Add sherry and parsley and stir well.

5. Cook uncovered for 5 minutes until sauce has reduced a little and become syrupy; the prawns should be heated through by now.

6. Add salt and pepper to taste and serve prawns immediately with the sauce.

Moules Marinières

Serves 2

2 oz/50 g butter

½ onion, chopped

½ – ¾ bottle (75cl) dry white wine

2 cloves of garlic, chopped

2 tbsp fresh parsley, finely chopped

3 lb/1.5 kg fresh mussels

4 fl oz/110 ml single cream

parsley to garnish

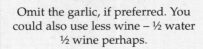

Omit the garlic, if preferred. You could also use less wine – ½ water ½ wine perhaps.

1. Wash the mussels well to remove any dirt. Make sure that each shell is closed before cooking. If not, discard them as they are dangerous to eat.

2. Melt the butter in a saucepan over a medium heat.

3. Add the onions and place the lid on the saucepan.

4. After a couple of minutes, add the wine and bring to the boil.

5. Add the garlic and the fresh parsley.

6. Add the mussels and stir into the sauce.

7. Next, add the cream and put the lid back on for a further 5 minutes on a high heat. Discard any unopened shells.

8. Serve in a shallow dish with a simple garnish of chopped parsley, and some crusty French bread.

Meat Dishes

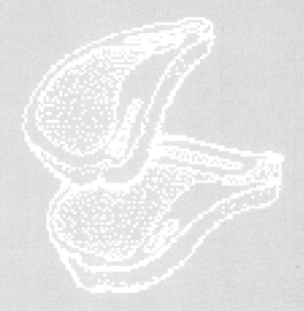

St. David's Lamb

Serves 1

1 oz/25 g butter

salt & pepper

3 lamb chops/cutlets (per person)

juice of half a lime

rind of half a lime, cut into strips

½ tsp green peppercorns

2 fl oz/50 ml dry white wine
(such as Pant-teg)

2 tsp balsamic vinegar

1. Heat a frying pan and melt ½ oz/15 g of the butter. Season chops before frying.

2. Cook chops for 3 minutes on each side until they have crisped slightly. Transfer to a plate and keep warm.

3. To make the sauce, add the lime juice and rind, peppercorns, wine and vinegar to the meat juices in the pan. Cook the sauce for 10 minutes until slightly reduced. Add a knob of butter to thicken sauce.

4. Return chops to the pan for a minute and heat through in the sauce.

5. Serve the chops with sauce poured over them.

Welsh Cawl

2 pts/1.2 l boiling water

1½ lbs/700 g lamb, cubed

1½ lbs/700 g potatoes, cubed

½ lb/225 g parsnips, chopped

½ lb/225 g turnips, chopped

½ lb/225 g carrots, chopped

1 large onion, chopped

½ savoy cabbage, shredded

2 leeks, finely chopped

4 tbsp parsley, finely chopped

salt & pepper

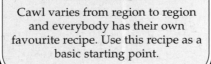

Cawl varies from region to region and everybody has their own favourite recipe. Use this recipe as a basic starting point.

1. Place the meat and vegetables – apart from the cabbage, and leeks – in the water and bring back to the boil.

2. Simmer for half an hour before skimming any fat from the surface of the broth.

3. Add remaining vegetables and cook for a further half an hour.

4. Add the parsley 10 minutes before the end of the cooking time.

5. Season well before serving.

Kleftico Exohiko

1. Wipe the meat with kitchen paper.

2. Heat the oil in a frying pan and seal meat quickly over a high heat, browning each side (cook for about 2-3 minutes).

3. Place the meat in a single layer on the bottom of a casserole dish.

4. Arrange vegetables over meat and sprinkle with remaining ingredients. Season well.

5. Cover dish with lid or foil to seal in steam.

6. Cook slowly for approximately 2-2½ hours until meat is tender: gas mark 3, 325°F/160°C.

Serves 6

6 lamb leg steaks, with bone (approximately 6-8 oz/175-225 g each)

1 tbsp olive oil

4 cloves garlic, crushed

1 medium onion, sliced

1 red pepper, sliced

1 green pepper, sliced

1 beef tomato, sliced

1 tsp dried oregano

1 tsp dried thyme

2-3 bayleaves

salt & pepper

Lamb with Rosemary

Serves 2

Rack of lamb (at least 6 chops)
salt & pepper
1 tbsp olive oil
3 sprigs rosemary
4 whole cloves garlic (optional)

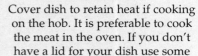

Cover dish to retain heat if cooking on the hob. It is preferable to cook the meat in the oven. If you don't have a lid for your dish use some foil.

Keep the cloves of garlic whole. The finer the garlic is chopped the stronger its flavour.

1. Season meat well before rubbing the olive oil over the rack of lamb.

2. Heat a large frying pan which will hold the meat comfortably.

3. Place meat in pan and brown gently. Cover the dish while meat is browning. (If you prefer your lamb pink, you can cook it uncovered in the oven for 15 minutes at gas mark 8, 450°F/230°C.)

4. Turn the meat and add rosemary.

5. Add the whole garlic cloves and replace cover.

6. Leave meat to cook for 15 minutes. If you prefer well-cooked meat, add a further 5-10 minutes' cooking time.

7. Serve with seasonal vegetables of your choice.

Lamb Kebabs

2 lbs/900 g fillet of lamb

3½ tsp fresh ginger, grated

3½ tsp soy sauce

3 tsp sesame oil

4 cloves garlic, crushed

salt & pepper

1. Trim fat from meat then cut into 1"/2.5 cm cubes.

2. Place meat in a shallow dish and add remaining ingredients. Mix well.

3. Cover bowl with foil or clingfilm and refrigerate for 12-48 hours. Stir every six hours or so.

4. Place meat on skewers, then barbecue or grill for 15-20 minutes.

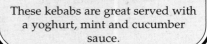

These kebabs are great served with a yoghurt, mint and cucumber sauce.

Pork Chops

1. Season the meat well.

2. Melt half an ounce of the butter in a frying pan and cook meat for 4 minutes. You could grill the chops if you prefer.

3. Slice the potatoes fairly thinly, then boil in salted water for 7-8 minutes. Don't over cook or they will disintegrate.

4. Place remaining butter and olive oil in a frying pan and add potatoes. Fry until golden brown.

5. Prepare additional vegetables to serve with the meal. Try to use different coloured vegetables, such as cauliflower and broccoli. This will make the meal a feast for the eyes as well as the stomach!

Serves 1

1 pork chop
salt & pepper, to taste
1½ oz/40 g butter
2 medium potatoes, peeled
1 tbsp olive oil

You could rub some soy sauce into the meat, then leave it to stand for an hour before cooking, or add garlic to the meat whilst cooking.

Remove the bone from the chop before cooking. If you can't do this, ask your butcher to do it for you.

Pork Stroganoff

Serves 2

1 tbsp sunflower oil

1 medium onion, sliced thinly

salt & pepper

8 oz/225 g pork fillet, cut into thin
strips

8 oz/225 g mushrooms (browncaps
or chestnuts)

1 red pepper, cut into strips

1 tbsp wholemeal flour

3 fl oz/75 ml white wine

3 fl oz/75 ml pork or chicken stock

1 tsp French mustard

1 tsp fresh thyme

5 fl oz/150 ml low fat natural
yoghurt

sprig of fresh thyme for decoration

*If you don't have any sunflower oil
then any vegetable oil will do.*

1. Heat oil in a large frying pan.

2. Fry onion over a low heat until softened.

3. Season pork well. Increase heat, add pork strips and fry quickly for 2-3 minutes.

4. Reduce heat and add sliced mushrooms and red pepper. Cook for a further 2 minutes. Add flour and stir well.

5. Remove from heat and add wine, stock, mustard and thyme.

6. Return to heat and bring to the boil, then allow to simmer for 10 minutes, uncovered. Stir frequently.

7. Remove from heat and allow to cool slightly; then add yoghurt and stir well.

8. Season well before garnishing with fresh thyme.

9. Serve with rice. Wild rice is very tasty and looks appetizing.

Pork with Smoky Bacon

1. Heat the oil and melt a little of the butter in a pan.

2. Add onion, lardons or bacon and pork. Fry lightly for about 8 minutes, stirring occasionally.

3. Add flour and stir well.

4. Add mushrooms and stock and stir well.

5. Finally, add paprika, soured cream, sausage, lemon juice and oregano. Stir well before transferring to a casserole dish.

6. Place in the oven and cook for 1 hour and 20 minutes at gas mark 4, 350°F/180°C.

7. Garnish with fresh parsley before serving.

Serves 4

1 tbsp olive oil

2 oz/50 g butter

1 onion, sliced

7 oz/200 g smoked lardons (or streaky bacon)

1 lb/450 g pork, cubed

2 tbsp wholemeal flour

12 mushrooms, quartered

½ pt/275 ml pork or chicken stock

1 tsp paprika

4 fl oz/110 ml soured cream

½ large pork sausage, sliced

juice of ½ lemon

2 tsp oregano

fresh parsley, finely chopped

Honeyed Ham in Peach Sauce

5-6 lbs/2.5-2.75 kg
piece of ham for boiling

3 tbsp honey

½ tbsp wholegrain mustard

1"/2.5 cm fresh ginger, grated

juice of an orange

rind of an orange, finely chopped

cloves (to stud ham)

Sauce:

1 tin (14 oz/400 g) sliced peaches
in syrup

1 glass sherry

1. In a bowl, stir together the honey, mustard, ginger, orange juice and rind.

2. Score the fat of the ham to form a diamond pattern. Then push a clove into the middle of each diamond. Place the ham in a roasting tin.

3. Pour honey mixture over the meat and bake for 3 hours 45 minutes, or until meat is browned, at gas mark 6, 400°F/ 200°C.

4. Remove ham from tin and set aside. Pour tinned peaches and sherry into roasting tin and heat thoroughly on the hob.

5. Carve meat and serve with the sauce.

Chilli Con Carne

Serves 4-6

3 tbsp oil

2 onions, chopped

4 cloves garlic, crushed

4 sticks celery, chopped

3 carrots, chopped

2 lbs/900 g minced beef

3 chopped chillies
(2 red & 1 green), or to taste

4 tbsp fresh coriander, finely
chopped

2 x 14 oz/400 g tinned tomatoes,
chopped

1 tin red kidney beans, drained

3 bay leaves

1 tbsp paprika

juice of a lime

2 tsp cumin

2 tbsp tomato purée

The chilli will taste even better if
left over night, then reheated the
following day.

1. Heat oil in a large pan and cook onions, garlic, celery and carrots until softened.

2. Add the minced beef and brown for 5-10 minutes before adding remaining ingredients, including the chillies. (Only you can decide the chilli strength required for the dish.)

3. Stir well and cook over a high heat for about 20 minutes, then reduce heat and cook for a further hour, ensuring that the chilli doesn't stick to the bottom of the pan.

Steak Chasseur

1. Melt butter in a frying pan.

2. Season meat before placing in pan.

3. Cook both steaks for 4 minutes on each side (for a medium cooked steak). You may alter the cooking time to achieve the steak you would prefer. Remove steak from pan and set aside.

4. In the same pan heat oil; add the onion and fry until softened. Then add mushrooms and stir-fry for 4-5 minutes.

5. Add wine, tomatoes, tarragon, parsley and brandy; take care if you decide to flame the brandy.

6. Add the stock or gravy and stir well for a minute or two, until sauce has thickened and is ready to serve.

1 oz/25 g unsalted butter

2 beef steaks, approximately 8 oz/225 g each

salt & pepper

1 tbsp oil

½ onion, sliced

8 oz/225 g mushrooms, sliced

2 glasses dry white wine

4 tomatoes or ½ tin tomatoes, finely chopped

2 tbsp tarragon, finely chopped

1 tbsp parsley, finely chopped

1 measure brandy (25 ml)

¼ pt/150 ml beef stock or gravy

If the sauce is too runny, cook for another few minutes to thicken.

Beef Wellington

2 tbsp oil

duxelle mix, which is 2 shallots, finely chopped and 2 oz/50 g mushrooms, finely chopped

8 oz/225 g beef fillet steak

8 oz/225 g pack puff pastry

1 oz/25 g good chicken liver pâté

salt & pepper

1 egg yolk

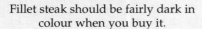

Fillet steak should be fairly dark in colour when you buy it.

Use shallots rather than onions as their flavour is milder.

Use oil rather than butter – it can withstand higher temperatures.

Don't use a pâté with too strong a flavour. You could replace it with mustard if preferred.

To ensure that there will be no blood left in the steak, bake it for 30 minutes.

1. Heat a spoonful of the oil in a frying pan.

2. Add shallots and mushrooms, and fry for a minute or two.

3. In another frying pan, heat a spoonful of the oil.

4. Place steak in pan. Seal for about a minute on each side. Remember that the steak will finish cooking in the pastry.

5. Place pastry on a board and roll out lightly. Spread a spoonful or two of the duxelle mixture over the pastry. Place meat on top and spread with pâté. Place the remaining duxelle mix on top of the meat. Seal the pastry to encase the meat.

6. Use the egg yolk to seal and glaze the pastry.

7. Bake in the oven for 20 minutes until pastry is golden and has risen: gas mark 6, 400°F/220°C.

8. Serve with seasonal vegetables.

Ostrich Steak

1 tbsp oil
½ onion, chopped
8 oz/225 g ostrich steak
salt & pepper

parsley to garnish

1. Heat the oil and fry the onion until golden.

2. Season the steak.

3. Fry the steak for 2 minutes each side until lightly browned.

4. As soon as the meat has browned, serve sprinkled with parsley and with a selection of vegetables or salad.

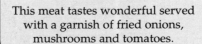

This meat tastes wonderful served with a garnish of fried onions, mushrooms and tomatoes.

Curry

1. Fry onions, garlic and ginger in a little of the butter until softened.

2. Add meat and fry until browned.

3. Add flour and a pinch of salt.

4. Add tomatoes and stir well. Add peppers and chillies.

5. Stir well and cook for 5-10 minutes.

6. Add curry powder and coconut milk (if desired) before stirring and cooking gently over a low heat for 15-20 minutes.

7. Transfer curry to a casserole dish, cover and cook for 30-45 minutes in the oven at gas mark 3, 325°F/160°C.

8. Serve with rice and a garnish of suitable fruit and vegetables.

Serves 4

2 oz/50 g butter

2 onions, chopped

4 cloves garlic, crushed

2"/5 cm ginger, grated

1 lb/450 g beef or skinless chicken, cubed

1 tbsp plain flour

1 x 14 oz/400 g tin tomatoes, chopped

½ each red, yellow and green pepper, sliced

2 red chillies, chopped

1 chopped green chilli (or to taste)

1-2 tbsp curry powder (Madras)

½ x 14 oz/400 g tin coconut milk (optional)

salt

Steak au Poivre

1 tsp olive oil
8 oz/225 g sirloin steak/rump steak
1 tsp black peppercorns
1 measure of brandy (25 ml)
2 tbsp beef stock
2 fl oz/55 ml double cream

parsley to garnish

Remember that the meat you choose should be dark red/ruby in colour.

Look for a marbling effect created by the fat in the meat. A little fat improves the texture and flavour of the meat.

Don't move the meat about whilst it is cooking. Turn the steak over once only, so as to keep the juices in.

Remember that peppercorns can taste very hot – especially black ones. If you're not too keen on a strong, peppery taste, opt for the green peppercorns as they are milder.

1. Pre-heat frying pan over a high heat source.

2. Crush the peppercorns. There's nothing worse than biting into a hard, whole peppercorn!

3. Rub some oil on the steak and press the peppercorns into the flesh.

4. Place the steak in the frying pan and cook for a minute each side. Remember to turn the meat once only, using a spatula.

5. Lift the steak on to a plate.

6. Then carefully add the brandy to the meat juices in the pan and flame. Next, add the cream and the beef stock.

7. Return the steak to the pan for a minute before serving on a plate with the sauce. Garnish with a little parsley.

Barbados Chicken

Serves 4

3 chicken breasts (skinless)

2 tbsp oil

1 medium onion, finely chopped

2 cloves garlic, crushed

2 whole red chillies

1"/2.5 cm fresh ginger, grated

1 red pepper, sliced

1 yellow pepper, sliced

8 mushrooms, sliced

½ fresh pineapple, peeled and chopped

2 glasses dry white wine

7 oz/200 g (½ tin) tomatoes

7 oz/200 g (½ tin) coconut milk

3 tbsp double cream

2 tbsp fresh coriander or 2 tsp dry coriander

salt & pepper

1 tbsp cornflour (optional)

1 tbsp water (optional)

slices of lime and fresh coriander

1. Cut the chicken breasts into quarters.

2. Heat the oil in a deep frying pan and cook the onion and garlic until soft.

3. Add the chicken and cook for 8-10 minutes.

4. Add the chillies, ginger, peppers and mushrooms. Cook for 5 minutes.

5. Add the pineapple, wine, tomatoes and coconut milk. Bring to the boil.

6. Simmer for 20 minutes until the meat has cooked through and the sauce has reduced a little.

7. Add the double cream, coriander and seasoning. You can thicken the sauce with a mixture of cornflour and water if you wish.

8. Serve with slices of lime and fresh coriander.

Chicken with Lime and Coriander

Serves 2

juice 1 lime

grated rind 1 lime

1 garlic clove, chopped

2½ tbsp fresh coriander, finely chopped

2 tbsp olive oil

1 tbsp white wine

1 tbsp runny honey

salt & pepper

2 skinless chicken breasts

1. Mix the lime juice, rind, garlic, coriander, oil, wine and honey in a bowl.

2. Add salt and pepper to taste, and mix once again.

3. Dip the chicken in the mixture before lifting onto a grill pan. Pour the remaining sauce over the chicken.

4. Cook under a hot grill for about 10 minutes each side.

5. Serve with vegetables or salad.

Use clear honey – its runny consistency blends easily with the other ingredients.

Take great care when cooking with honey – it can burn easily due to its high sugar content.

Grill temperatures vary considerably, so cooking times should be adjusted accordingly.

Chicken with Avocado

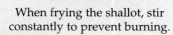
1. Melt the butter in a frying pan.

2. Add the chicken and fry for about 2 minutes. Sprinkle with salt and pepper.

3. Turn the meat over and cook for a further 8 minutes or so. Cover the pan with foil (or a lid) to keep the steam in.

4. Remove the chicken from the pan and place on a plate while you prepare the sauce.

5. Fry the shallot slowly and then add the wine. Mix well.

6. Add the cream and tarragon. Cook for 5 minutes.

7. Slice the chicken carefully – you should have about 7 slices from each piece.

8. Peel and slice the avocado.

9. Alternate the chicken and the avocado slices and serve with the sauce on the side of the plate.

Turkey Meatballs with Cranberry Sauce

Serves 6

For the sauce:

4 oz/110 g cranberries

4 tsp sherry

2 tbsp oil

2 tbsp brown sugar

7-8 drops tabasco sauce

For the turkey balls:

1 lb/450 g cooked turkey mince

2 oz/50 g toasted walnuts, ground

1 tbsp Parmesan cheese

1 tbsp olive oil

3 sticks of celery, finely chopped

2 garlic cloves, finely chopped

2 tbsp cranberry sauce or jelly

½ tsp cumin

½ tsp oregano

½ tsp coriander

salt & pepper to taste

2 eggs

4 oz/110 g breadcrumbs

oil for deep-frying

1. Mix the sauce ingredients in a saucepan. Then cook over a medium heat for 5 minutes, making sure all of the brown sugar has melted. Set aside.

2. Mix the turkey mince, the walnuts and the Parmesan cheese together in a bowl.

3. Heat the oil and cook the celery for 2 minutes.

4. Add the remaining ingredients – apart from the eggs and breadcrumbs – and cook for about 5 minutes.

5. Add this mixture to the turkey mix and shape into balls. Dip the turkey balls into the beaten eggs and cover with breadcrumbs before deep-frying them in vegetable oil.

6. When they have browned, lift the turkey balls from the oil and place on kitchen paper.

7. Before you bring the dish to the table, pour the sauce over the turkey balls.

Chicken Wings in Garlic

Serves 2

1 tsp coriander seeds
½ tsp cumin seeds
¼ tsp fennel seeds
2 or 3 large garlic cloves
½ tsp salt
juice 2 lemons
2 tbsp olive oil
12 chicken wings

1. To improve the flavour of the herbs, toast the coriander, cumin and fennel seeds in a small frying pan for approximately 1-1½ minutes until they begin to brown. Remember to turn them constantly.

2. Pour the seeds into a mortar and crush with a pestle. Add the garlic and salt and grind them into the seeds for 1-2 minutes.

3. Add the lemon juice and oil and mix together.

4. Place the chicken wings in a bowl and cover with the mixture. Leave to stand for 5-6 hours, remembering to turn them over now and again.

5. Transfer the wings into an ovenproof dish and cook for 30 minutes at gas mark 6, 400°F/200°C. Then, lift them onto a baking tray and cook for a further 10 minutes, making sure that they become light brown all over.

Pasta & Rice Dishes

Vegetable Lasagne

Serves 4

4 tbsp olive oil

2 garlic cloves, crushed

1 onion, finely chopped

3 sticks of celery, sliced

14 oz/400 g tin chopped tomatoes

2 tbsp tomato purée

2 courgettes, sliced

salt & pepper to taste

15 sheets of lasagne pasta

8 oz/225 g Mozzarella cheese

1. For the sauce, fry the onion and garlic in the olive oil until they are lightly browned.

2. Add the celery and cook for 5 minutes.

3. Next, add the tomatoes, tomato purée, salt and pepper. Cook for 5-10 minutes.

4. In a separate frying pan, fry the courgettes for 2 minutes before adding them to the rest of the mixture.

5. Fill an ovenproof dish with layers of sauce, layers of pasta and layers of cheese, making sure you have a layer of pasta on the top. Sprinkle generously with cheese before placing the dish in the oven to cook for 30 minutes on gas mark 4, 350°F/180°C.

Pasta with Garlic and Herbs

1. Cook the pasta for approximately 9-12 minutes in boiling, salted water containing 1 tablespoon of oil.

2. Mix the herbs together in a bowl and add the fromage frais and garlic.

3. When the pasta is ready, drain and add to the bowl of fromage frais, garlic and herbs. Mix them well. Add the salt and pepper before serving.

Serves 2-3

14 oz/400 g fusilli pasta

1 tbsp olive oil

2 tbsp fresh parsley, finely chopped

1 tbsp fresh oregano, finely chopped

2 tbsp fresh thyme, finely chopped

8 oz/225 g fromage frais

1 garlic clove, crushed

salt & pepper to taste

Tagliatelle Carbonara

tagliatelle pasta
pinch of salt
1 oz/25 g butter
pepper
2 garlic cloves, finely chopped
2 slices ham
2 fl oz/55 ml single cream
6 fresh basil leaves,
roughly chopped

Parmesan cheese

Remember, if you cut the ham into pieces that are too small you will lose its flavour.

When the pasta is ready, pour some cold water over it to stop any further cooking, and also to prevent it from sticking together. (The same applies to rice.)

It's easier to cut basil if you roll the leaf tightly first of all. Always use a sharp knife! Dried basil may be used as a substitute, but remember that you won't need half as much.

1. Cook the pasta in a pan of boiling, slightly salted water. Run some cold water into the saucepan until the pasta has cooled. Strain the pasta and set to one side.

2. Melt some butter in a saucepan and add the pepper and garlic.

3. Cut the ham into squares and add to the saucepan, mixing well.

4. Next, add the cream and heat gently, making sure not to turn the heat too high.

5. Add the pasta and heat through in the sauce before adding the basil.

6. Serve with some Parmesan cheese.

Paella

1. Leave the saffron to stand in 2 tablespoons of boiling water.

2. Melt the butter in a deep frying pan, or a paella pan.

3. Add the bacon, garlic and onion and cook over a medium heat until they are lightly browned.

4. Add the rice and the saffron.

5. After removing the bones and the skin from the chicken, cut the meat into four pieces.

6. Add the meat to the rice along with the tomatoes and stock, and mix together well.

7. Let the mixture simmer in the pan – without a lid on – for 20 minutes on a low heat, turning frequently so that the rice does not catch and burn.

8. Add the remaining ingredients and cook everything for a further 10 minutes until the shells of the moules are open, and all the liquid has been absorbed.

9. Season with salt and pepper and serve the paella garnished with wedges of lemon.

Serves 4

pinch of saffron (optional)
2 tbsp boiling water
2 oz/50 g butter
4 slices bacon, cut into small pieces
2 garlic cloves, crushed
1 medium onion, finely chopped
8 oz/225 g long grain rice
1 lb/450 g chicken, cooked
14 oz/400 g tin chopped tomatoes
½ pint/275 ml chicken stock
7 oz/200 g tin of tuna, drained
5 oz/150 g cooked moules (without their shells)
6 moules, in shells
6 king prawns
5 oz/150 g pickled prawns
salt & pepper

wedges of lemon to garnish

Pasta Carla

Serves 4

4 veal escalopes

8 tsp pesto

4 slices Parma ham

8 dried tomatoes

2 tbsp olive oil

1 garlic clove, sliced

mixed wild mushrooms for the garnish

2 fl oz/55 ml Marsala wine

1 lb/450 g tagliatelle

2 tsp pesto

2 tbsp double cream, whipped

1 sprig of basil

Parmesan cheese for the garnish

Ragu sauce for the garnish

salt & pepper

1. Place the escalopes flat on the table and then spread 2 teaspoons of pesto over each one. On top of this, place a slice of Parma ham and 2 dried tomatoes for each escalope.

2. Roll the escalopes tightly and wrap with separate pieces of greaseproof paper to form neat parcels.

3. Cook the escalopes for approximately 10 minutes in a pressure cooker and leave to stand for about 5 minutes before removing the greaseproof paper and slicing the meat thinly.

4. Heat some oil in a frying pan and cook the garlic until soft. Then add the mushrooms and cook for 2-3 minutes before adding the Marsala wine. Cook the mixture for a further 1 minute. Remove the mushrooms from the pan and keep warm so that they may be used to garnish the dish.

5. Cook the pasta in boiling, salted water for approximately 9-12 minutes.

6. For the sauce, add the 2 teaspoons of pesto to the other ingredients in the frying pan and pour the whipped cream into it. Stir, and cook for 2-3 minutes.

7. When the pasta has cooked, drain well and serve a portion on each plate. Pour the sauce around the pasta and add the mushrooms; then place some slices of veal on the pasta.

8. Garnish with a sprig of basil and very thin slices of Parmesan cheese. To add colour to the dish, use a piping bag to pipe 12 dots of Ragu sauce on top of the cream and basil sauce, and then drag the blade of a knife through the middle of each dot to create a heart shape.

Vegetables & Vegetarian Dishes

French Salad

Serves 4

4 oz lardons (or thick cut streaky bacon)

8 oz/225 g cooked new potatoes

2 diced tomatoes

1 diced red pepper

1 lettuce, roughly torn

1 hard boiled egg, cut into quarters

For the dressing:

1 tbsp Dijon mustard

1 tbsp white wine vinegar or raspberry vinegar

1 shallot, finely chopped

salt & pepper to taste

olive oil

1. Wash the lettuce and dry well.

2. Fry the lardons until light brown.

3. Cut the potatoes in half if they are too big.

4. Add the potatoes to the frying pan with the lardons and cook for 2-3 minutes until they are slightly golden, and leave to cool.

5. Prepare the dressing in a small bowl: mix the mustard, vinegar and shallot together and season with salt and pepper.

6. Whisk the oil into the mixture gradually.

7. Put the tomatoes, red pepper, lettuce and egg in a large bowl, together with the lardons and potatoes.

8. Pour the dressing over the salad.

9. Serve immediately with crusty French bread.

Caesar Salad

1. Wash the lettuce leaves and dry well. Tear into small pieces and return to the fridge for half an hour before using them.

2. Remove the crusts from the bread and then cut the bread into small squares.

3. Fry the bread in a frying pan with the butter and oil until it is lightly browned.

4. Drain the oil from the anchovies and cut them into half inch pieces.

5. When you are ready to eat the salad, place the lettuce in a bowl, add the croutons, the anchovies and the sliced boiled egg.

6. Mix the ingredients for the dressing. After pouring the dressing over the salad, sprinkle some Parmesan cheese over the top and serve with crusty French bread.

Serves 2

7 oz/200 g mixed lettuce leaves
2 slices bread
1 tbsp olive oil
2 oz/50 g butter
1 oz/25 g anchovies
1 hard-boiled egg (7 minutes)
1 tbsp Parmesan cheese

For the dressing:
1 tbsp olive oil
1 tbsp lemon juice
1 garlic clove, crushed
salt & pepper

Vegetarian Sunday Lunch

Serves 1

1 aubergine

1 courgette

oil or butter to cook

½ onion

1 garlic clove, crushed

3 beef tomatoes

2 glasses dry white wine

salt & pepper

fresh coriander

juice of ½ a lemon

6 asparagus

2 tsp pine kernels

2 tsp yoghurt

1. Cut the aubergine and courgette lengthways into long, thick strips and place on a plate. Sprinkle a little salt over them and leave to sweat for approximately 15 minutes.

2. Cut a thick slice off one of the beef tomatoes and set to one side.

3. For the sauce, heat some oil or butter in a saucepan and cook the onions and garlic until soft. After de-seeding and peeling the tomatoes, add them to the onions in the pan. Then, add some wine and salt and pepper and let the sauce reduce before adding the fresh coriander and lemon juice.

4. Heat the frying pan. Before cooking the courgettes and aubergine lightly in a little butter or oil, dry them off with kitchen paper.

5. Next, add the slice of tomato to the frying pan, browning both sides.

6. Cook the asparagus in boiling salted water for approximately 5-7 minutes.

7. Cook the pine kernels in a little butter and 5 fl oz/150 ml of water for 2-3 minutes.

8. Pour a little of the sauce on a large plate. Arrange 4 slices of aubergine alternating with 4 slices of courgette around the plate and place the tomato slice in the centre. Add a little yoghurt to each piece of aubergine and create an attractive pattern with the asparagus and pine kernels.

Cheese Fondue

1. Rub around the inside of the fondue pot with the cut clove of garlic.

2. Grate the cheese fairly coarsely.

3. Blend the cornflour with the kirsch until smooth and set aside.

4. Heat the wine and the lemon juice in the pot until just boiling; next, turn the heat down and stir in the cheese very slowly with a wooden spoon.

5. Add the kirsch mixture, pepper and nutmeg, stirring continuously until it thickens. The cheese mixture should be smooth – stir in a little more warmed wine if necessary.

6. Transfer the pot to a spirit stove or electric hot plate at the table and keep it simmering. The fondue is now ready to eat with the crusty bread cubes. Remember to stir the pot frequently during the meal. Do not let the fondue boil.

7. When nearly all the fondue has been eaten, there will be a thick crust on the bottom of the pot, and this should be scraped and divided between the guests.

Serves 4-6

1 garlic clove, cut in half
12 oz/350 g Emmental cheese
12 oz/350 g Gruyère cheese
2 tbsp/30 ml kirsch
2 tsp cornflour
15 fl oz/425 ml dry white wine
2 tsp/10 ml lemon juice
a pinch of freshly ground white pepper
a pinch of freshly grated nutmeg
1 large loaf of crusty bread, cut into 1"/2.5 cm cubes

A side dish of pickled onions and gherkins is usually served with cheese fondue. If you are serving a dessert to follow it, choose a simple fruit salad or a bowl of fresh fruit.

Glazed Carrots in an Orange Sauce

1 oz/25 g butter

1 lb/450 g carrots, cut into strips

½ orange rind, sliced and finely chopped

juice of 1 orange

2 tsp brown sugar

salt & pepper

1. Melt the butter in a saucepan.

2. Add the carrots, the juice and rind of the orange and mix together well before adding the brown sugar and seasoning.

3. Place a lid over the saucepan and cook for 5-10 minutes until the carrots are tender.

Creamy Leeks with Almonds

1 oz/25 g butter

½ onion, sliced

1 large leek, chopped into ½"/1 cm cubes

salt & pepper

½ small carton double cream

flaked almonds, lightly toasted

1. Melt the butter in a large frying pan, then add the onion and the leek and season; cook for 3 minutes before adding the cream.

2. Cook for a further 2-3 minutes until the cream begins to thicken.

3. Before serving, sprinkle with some flaked almonds.

Red Cabbage in Wine

1. Melt the butter in a pan, add the onions and garlic and fry for 2 minutes before adding the red cabbage.

2. Cook for a further 2 minutes and then add the wine.

3. Leave to cook on a medium heat for 3-4 minutes and add salt and pepper to taste.

1 oz/25 g butter
½ onion, sliced
2 garlic cloves, finely chopped
½ red cabbage, thinly cut
4 fl oz/110 ml white wine
salt & pepper

Stuffed Tomatoes

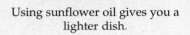

Serves 2

4 large tomatoes (beef if possible)

1 tbsp sunflower oil

1 medium onion, finely chopped

1 large mushroom, sliced

1 lemon, juice and grated rind

1 tsp cumin seeds

1 tbsp ground nuts

2 tbsp fresh mint, finely chopped

8 oz/225 g of cooked brown
or white rice

salt & pepper

1-2 tsp Parmesan cheese

Greek yoghurt

mint leaves to garnish

Using sunflower oil gives you a
lighter dish.

1. Slice the top off each of the tomatoes and set to one side.

2. Spoon out the inside of the tomatoes with a teaspoon.

3. Heat some oil in a frying pan, or a wok if you prefer, and fry the onion until soft, but not brown.

4. Add the sliced mushroom, the grated zest and juice of one lemon, the cumin seeds, nuts and mint and cook for a further 4-5 minutes.

5. Add the rice and mix well with the other ingredients; cook for 4-5 minutes, remembering to turn the mixture frequently.

6. Add the salt and pepper and leave the mixture to cool a little.

7. Fill the tomatoes with the mixture and place in a casserole dish, without the lid on, before sprinkling them with Parmesan cheese.

8. Cook the tomatoes for 10-15 minutes until they are soft and their crowns lightly browned: gas mark 4, 350°F/ 180°C. (Make sure that you don't overcook the tomatoes as this will split the skins.)

9. The tomatoes may be served with Greek yoghurt and garnished with mint leaves and the lid of each tomato.

Tomatoes with Spinach

1. Slice the top off each tomato and spoon out the inside, making sure not to cut through their skins.

2. Wash the spinach and place directly in a saucepan. Cook for 2-3 minutes over a medium heat, turning frequently until the spinach is soft.

3. Leave the spinach to drain well before chopping it into small pieces. Mix with the nutmeg, yoghurt and salt and pepper.

4. Set aside a few shallot rings and add the rest to the spinach, mixing well.

5. Fill the tomatoes with the mixture.

6. Mix the breadcrumbs and cheese together and sprinkle over the tomatoes.

7. Place the tomatoes in a shallow dish and cook for 12-15 minutes on gas mark 3, 325°F/160°C until the tomatoes have softened. Do not overcook.

8. Serve with the shallot rings.

Serves 2

4 large tomatoes
8 oz/225 g fresh spinach
½ tbsp freshly grated nutmeg
2 tbsp Greek yoghurt, drained
salt & pepper
2 shallots, sliced into rings
1 tbsp toasted breadcrumbs
1 tbsp grated Parmesan cheese

Puddings

Welsh Cakes

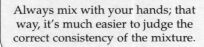

1 lb/450 g plain flour
4 oz/110 g sugar
1 tsp cream of tartar
1 tsp bicarbonate of soda
4 oz/110 g lard
4 oz/110 g margarine
8 oz/225 g currants
2 eggs
2 tbsp water
caster sugar

1. Sift the flour into a bowl and then add the sugar, the cream of tartar and bicarbonate of soda. Rub in the lard and margarine until the mixture resembles fine breadcrumbs.

2. Stir in the currants.

3. Lightly whisk the eggs before adding them to the dry mixture. Next, add the water and mix together well. Set aside for half an hour.

4. Roll out the mixture on a floured surface and then cut out 2½"/6 cm rounds.

5. Heat and grease the hotplate. Cook the Welsh cakes on the plate until lightly browned, and then turn over. Alternatively, you can use a heavy frying pan.

6. Dust with a little caster sugar and leave to cool before serving.

Always mix with your hands; that way, it's much easier to judge the correct consistency of the mixture.

Hot Cross Buns

1 lb/450 g strong white plain flour

1 tsp salt

6 oz/175 g dried mixed fruit

1 tsp mixed spice

2 oz/50 g caster sugar

1 oz/25 g fresh yeast (or 2 tbsp dried yeast)

8 fl oz/225 ml milk and warm water
(+ 2 extra tbsp)

2 oz/50 g butter or margarine

1 egg

For the crosses and glaze:

1½ oz/40 g plain flour

4 tbsp water

4 oz/100 g sugar

6 tbsp milk

1. Rub the flour and butter together, and then add the mixed fruit, salt and spices in a medium-sized bowl.

2. In a small bowl, mix the sugar, yeast and the 2 tablespoons of milk and warm water. Set aside and let the yeast work.

3. In another bowl, beat the egg and add to it the yeast and the 8 fl oz of milk and water mixture.

4. Next, add the wet mixture to the dry mixture.

5. After mixing all the ingredients well, knead the dough until smooth and elastic, for about 5 minutes. Shape into balls.

6. For the crosses, form a paste from the flour and water and use a piping bag to pipe on the crosses.

7. Cover the buns with a clean, dry cloth and leave in a warm place for about an hour until they have doubled in size.

8. Cook the buns for about 20 minutes in a warm oven: gas mark 6, 400°F/200°C.

9. For an attractive glaze, bring some sugar and milk to the boil and brush over the buns whilst they are still hot from the oven.

Bread and Butter Pudding

1. Spread some butter on the bread slices and cut them in to three pieces (remove the crusts if you wish).

2. Place a layer of the bread and butter (approximately half) over the base of an ovenproof dish. Sprinkle with the white sugar and sultanas and then cover with the remaining pieces of bread.

3. Mix the eggs well and add the milk to them, before mixing once again. Pour the mixture over the bread and leave to stand for 15-20 minutes. Sprinkle the top with a little brown sugar.

4. Cook in the oven for 35-40 minutes on gas mark 3, 325°F/160°C until the pudding is golden.

Serves 4

6 slices white bread
softened butter
1 oz/25 g sugar
2 tbsp sultanas
2 eggs
¾ pint/425 ml milk
1-2 tbsp brown sugar

Crêpes Suzette

4 oz/110 g plain flour
½ pint/275 ml milk
1 egg
½ oz/15 g melted butter
pinch of salt
oil to cook

For the sauce:
3 oz/75 g butter
3 tbsp soft brown sugar
2 tbsp brandy
2-3 tbsp Grand Marnier
8 fl oz/225 ml orange juice

1. In a large bowl, mix the flour and milk together well.

2. Add the egg, salt and melted butter and mix once again.

3. Leave the mixture in the fridge for 30 minutes before you are ready to use it.

4. For each pancake, heat ½ a teaspoon of the oil at a time in a frying pan.

5. Cook the pancakes (make sure they are thin) and set aside.

6. For the sauce, melt the butter in the frying pan and add the sugar.

7. Mix well, making sure all the sugar has melted. Remember not to turn the heat too high.

8. Add the brandy and the Grand Marnier and flame carefully.

9. Add the orange juice – if possible, use the juice of freshly squeezed oranges.

10. Cook the sauce for 10 minutes before placing the pancakes in the sauce one by one, and then folding them into quarters.

11. Once all the pancakes have been folded, heat in the pan for a further 5 minutes.

Christmas Parcels

4 oz/110 g cream cheese

3 oz/75 g glacé cherries, sliced

3 tbsp mincemeat

2 oz/50 g peeled and grated apple

grated orange peel

24 pieces filo pastry cut
into 6"/15 cm squares

2 oz/50 g melted butter

icing sugar to decorate

1. Mix the cream cheese, cherries, mincemeat, apple and the orange peel together in a bowl.

2. Take one piece of filo pastry; brush with some melted butter and place another piece of pastry on top. Brush again with melted butter.

3. Place a third piece of pastry on top of that one and turn the edges so as to form a star shape.

4. Brush with some melted butter and place yet another piece of pastry on top of the third piece. (Remember to cover the rest of the pastry in case it becomes dry.)

5. Take a spoonful of the mincemeat mixture and put some in the middle of the pastry.

6. Bring the corners of the pastry together to form a parcel.

7. Repeat steps 2-6 until you have used all the pastry.

8. Brush the parcels with the melted butter and place on a baking sheet in the oven for 20 minutes until they are a light brown colour: gas mark 6, 400°F/200°C.

9. Sprinkle the parcels with a generous dusting of icing sugar and serve warm.

Peach Crumble

1. Place the peaches in boiling water for a few seconds, then plunge into cold water.

2. Peel off the skins, cut the fruit in half, then stone and roughly chop.

3. Place the fruit in a shallow, ovenproof dish and add the orange juice, sherry and honey.

4. Mix together the biscuits, sultanas, ginger, margarine and almonds (setting aside 1 tablespoon of the nuts).

5. Sprinkle the mixture over the peaches and place in the oven at gas mark 5, 375°C/190°F for 15-20 minutes.

6. Sprinkle the crumble with the remaining almonds and serve.

Serves 4

5 ripe peaches
3 tbsp orange juice
1 tbsp sweet sherry
2 tbsp clear honey
5 oz/150 g muesli biscuits, crushed
1 oz/25 g sultanas
½ tsp ground ginger
10 oz/25 g margarine, melted

2 oz/50 g chopped almonds

Mincemeat Roulade

4 eggs (separated)

4 oz/110 g sugar (caster)

8 oz/225 g mincemeat

4 tbsp sifted flour

¼ pint/150 ml of double cream

25 ml rum or brandy

icing sugar (to decorate)

1. Beat the egg yolks and sugar until the consistency is thick and mousse-like.

2. Beat the egg whites until stiff, but not dry.

3. Fold the egg yolk mixture into the mincemeat and sifted flour. Then, using a tablespoon, fold in the whites carefully.

4. Spread the mixture into a 12" x 8"/30 cm x 20 cm Swiss roll tin lined with greaseproof paper.

5. Bake for 10-15 minutes in a pre-heated oven: gas mark 4, 350°F/180°C.

6. Cover your wire rack with a clean, damp cloth. Turn out the cake onto the cloth – the underside facing upwards. Then, place a clean, dry cloth over the cake and leave it to cool for 10 minutes before peeling off the greaseproof paper.

7. Transfer onto some greaseproof paper sprinkled with icing sugar. Lightly whip the cream in a bowl. Next, stir in the rum or brandy and spread evenly over the roulade.

8. Use the greaseproof paper to lift one end of the roulade and then roll it carefully; sift some icing sugar over the surface just before serving.

Dudley's Pick-'n'-Mix Gâteau

3 layers of sponge cake 10"/25 cm

apricot jam

1 pint/570 ml double cream, whipped

½ lb/225 g strawberries (cut in half)

1 mango, sliced thinly

4 tbsp kirsch

7 oz/200 g roasted flaked almonds

1. Spread some jam over one layer of sponge, and then some cream. Arrange a circle of strawberries on the edge of the sponge and cover the rest with the sliced mango.

2. Place the second layer of sponge directly on top of the first, spoon some kirsch on the surface and repeat step one with the fruit and cream.

3. Place the last layer of sponge on top and cover it with cream.

4. Use some more of the cream to spread over the sides of the gâteau.

5. Press the almonds on the side of the cake and decorate the top with the remainder of the mango, strawberries and cream.

Gâteau Mille Feuilles

1. Once you have rolled the pastry, divide into three equal rectangles and place on a baking tray in the oven for 10 minutes on gas mark 4, 350°F/180°C. Leave to cool.

2. Whip the cream and icing sugar in a bowl; add the crème pâtissière and mix together well.

3. Cut the strawberries into pieces, setting aside some of the fruit to decorate the gâteau.

4. On one pastry rectangle, spread the jam, then the cream mixture and then the fruit containing some Cointreau.

5. Place the second layer of pastry on top and repeat step 4 twice.

6. Cover the gâteau with the remaining cream. Lightly press the almonds on the sides of the gâteau and then sift some icing sugar on top. Decorate with strawberries.

1 pack 8 oz/225 g puff pastry
1 pint/570 ml whipping cream
6 oz/175 g icing sugar
4 tbsp crème pâtissière
½ lb / 225 g strawberries (or any fruit of your choice)
4 tbsp strawberry jam
2 fl oz/55 ml Cointreau
7 oz/200 g packet flaked almonds

icing sugar to decorate

Fruit Slice

1 pack 8 oz/225 g puff pastry

1 pt/570 ml double cream

13 oz/375 g mixed fruit – eg strawberries, raspberries, blackcurrants etc.

icing sugar – enough to cover the top of the fruit slice

3½ oz/100 g flaked almonds

1. Roll the puff pastry until fairly thin and then divide into 3 equal rectangles. Prick the pastry all over with a fork before transferring on to a baking tray. Cook in the oven for 10-15 minutes on gas mark 4, 350°F/180°C. Leave to cool.

2. Whip the cream and spoon into a piping bag. Pipe the cream over the surface of one piece of pastry and then add a layer of fruit.

3. Place the next piece of pastry on top of the fruit and then repeat the process until the last piece of pastry is in place.

4. Pipe some more cream, ensuring that the whole slice is covered.

5. Cover the sides of the fruit slice with flaked almonds and sprinkle a generous helping of icing sugar on top. If you have a metal skewer, heat it and then make a criss-cross pattern on top of the slice, melting the icing sugar.

Walnut Galette

2 oz/50 g caster sugar
9 oz/250 g margarine
12 oz/350 g self-raising flour
9 oz/250 g chopped walnuts
3 medium apples, stewed
2 oz/50 g sultanas
6 oz/175 g dark brown sugar
1 tsp mixed spice
1 pint/570 ml whipped cream

1. Beat the sugar and margarine well in a bowl.

2. Add the flour and 8 oz/225 g of the nuts and mix to form a dough. Leave to stand in the fridge for half an hour.

3. Divide the mixture into two equal parts and roll the 2 halves into circles. Cover one of the circles with the remaining walnuts (this will be the top half of the galette).

4. Transfer the two halves on to a baking tray and place in the oven for 15-20 minutes: gas mark 4, 350°F/180°C.

5. After they have cooled a little, lift them on to a wire rack and leave for about half an hour.

6. Using a serrated knife, cut the upper half of the galette into quarters – take care, as the crust may crumble easily – and then cut the quarters into 3 smaller slices. Next, take a scone cutter and cut a circle from the centre of this top circle.

7. Mix the stewed apples, sultanas, brown sugar and mixed spice together well, and spread the mixture over the second half of the galette.

8. Using a piping bag, pipe some cream over the apple mixture.

9. Arrange the crust slices on top of the cream to resemble a clock.

10. Decorate the galette with a rosette of cream.

Banana and Rum Pudding

1. Melt the butter in a frying pan, taking care not to let it burn.

2. Add the sugar and mix well until the sugar has melted.

3. When the sugar is bubbling, add the bananas and cinnamon, and stir for 2 minutes over a low heat.

4. Add the rum and the banana liqueur, and then flame the rum carefully.

5. Mix together and serve immediately.

Serves 4

4 oz/110 g unsalted butter
4 oz/110 g soft muscovado sugar
6 bananas, sliced in half
½ tsp cinnamon
banana liqueur, if available
3½ fl oz/100 ml dark rum

Don't worry if the mixture looks as if it's separating after you add the bananas; the rum will give it a treacle-like consistency.

Alpine Apples

1. Heat the oven to gas mark 4, 350°F/180°C.

2. Wash and core the apples, then score the peel about two-thirds of the way up the sides of the apples.

3. Beat the egg whites until soft peaks form and then mix in the nuts and sugar.

4. Place the apples in an ovenproof dish and fill them with the egg mixture. Melt the butter in a pan and pour it over and around the apples.

5. Bake the apples until soft – for approximately 40-45 minutes – basting them occasionally with the butter in the dish. Be careful not to overcook the apples as they will split. If they brown too quickly, cover them with buttered greaseproof paper.

6. Serve the apples hot with cream or custard.

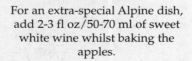

For an extra-special Alpine dish, add 2-3 fl oz/50-70 ml of sweet white wine whilst baking the apples.

Strawberries in Cointreau and Cream

8 oz/200 g strawberries
2 tbsp icing sugar
2 fl oz/55 ml Cointreau
6 fl oz/175 ml double cream

1. Place the strawberries in a bowl and add the Cointreau and icing sugar. Leave the ingredients to chill for 45 minutes in the fridge.

2. Add the double cream and mix everything together. Return the bowl to the fridge.

3. Take the pudding out of the fridge 20 minutes before you are ready to serve it.

Strawberry Pudding

1. Beat the egg yolk well with a whisk for about 10 minutes until the mixture thickens and becomes pale yellow in colour.

2. Pour the water and lemon juice into a saucepan, add the sugar and rhubarb, and bring to the boil; continue boiling for a further 3 minutes. Strain the rhubarb pieces and let them cool.

3. Add the rhubarb syrup to the egg yolk, but be careful not to let it come into contact with the whisk or the sides of the bowl as it will harden immediately and spoil the mixture. Also remember not to add too much of the syrup at once, as the heat will cook the egg.

4. Add the cream to the mixture, mixing carefully with a large spoon.

5. Arrange the rhubarb and strawberries neatly on a plate. Cover the fruit with a little of the sauce and icing sugar.

6. Before serving, place the pudding under the grill on a high heat until the sauce is golden in colour.

(Remember, use a heat-proof plate and keep an eye on the pudding in case it burns.)

1 egg yolk

4½ fl oz/130 ml water

juice of ½ lemon

4½ oz/130 g sugar

10 oz/275 g rhubarb, cut into 1"/2.5 cm pieces

¼ pint/150 ml whipped cream

10 oz/275 g strawberries

icing sugar to decorate

Quick Raspberry and Banana Sorbet

1 large or 2 small bananas

8 oz/225 g frozen raspberries

2 sprigs fresh mint to garnish

1. Place the banana and the unthawed raspberries into a food processor and liquidize for 2-3 minutes until the fruit has been puréed.

2. Spoon the mixture into small individual bowls, garnish with the mint and serve.

Soft Fruits in a Caramel Crust

4 oz/110 g strawberries

4 oz/110 g raspberries

2 tbsp caster sugar

2 fl oz/55 ml kirsch

9 oz/250 g mascarpone cheese

4 oz/110 g light brown muscovado sugar

1. Cut the strawberries in half and place in a bowl, together with the raspberries.

2. Pour the caster sugar over the fruit and then the kirsch. Mix together well and leave in the fridge for an hour.

3. Next, transfer the fruit into small, individual ramekins and leave a gap of ½" (1 cm) from the top of the dishes.

4. Spoon some mascarpone cheese on top of the fruit (approximately one tablespoon for each ramekin), and press down, making sure the surface of the cheese is even.

5. Sprinkle a generous helping of brown sugar on top of the cheese and place the ramekins under the grill for 5 minutes until the sugar has caramelized.

Strawberry Ice Cream

2 lb/900 g strawberries
1 lb/450 g icing sugar
1 pint/570 ml double cream
1 tbsp lemon juice

1. Blend the strawberries and icing sugar in a liquidizer until smooth.

2. Pour the mixture into a bowl and add the cream and lemon juice and stir well.

3. If you have an ice cream maker, spoon the mixture into it and leave for 20 minutes. Alternatively, transfer the mixture into a plastic container and place in the freezer. Remember to stir every 30 minutes until frozen.

Tiramisù

Serves 6

4 egg yolks

3 oz/75 g caster sugar

8 oz/225 g Mascarpone cheese

4 fl oz/100 ml double cream
(lightly whipped)

3 egg whites

¼ pint/150 ml strong expresso
coffee

3 tbsp rum or brandy

Two 7 oz/200 g packs
sponge fingers

2 oz/50 g grated dark continental
chocolate

1 dsp cocoa powder

*This dessert may also be prepared
in individual glasses.*

1. Beat the egg yolks and sugar until the mixture thickens and becomes pale in colour.

2. Mix together the cheese and the lightly whipped cream in another bowl and then add carefully to the sugar and egg yolks little by little, beating the mixture well with each addition.

3. In yet another separate bowl, whisk the egg whites until they form soft peaks. Then lightly fold into the cream mixture.

4. Mix the coffee and rum or brandy in a shallow dish.

5. Dip the sponge fingers into the coffee mixture then place half the sponges on the base of a large glass bowl.

6. Spread a layer of the cream mixture over the sponge, then sprinkle some grated chocolate on top.

7. Repeat the process until you have filled the bowl, ending with a layer of the cream mixture.

8. Sieve some cocoa powder over this layer and add any chocolate you may have left.

9. Chill in the fridge for at least 4 hours – or overnight – to enhance the flavour.

Marmalade Ice Cream

4 oz/110 g caster sugar

9 fl oz/250 ml water

1 tbsp lemon juice

4 tbsp marmalade

10 fl oz/275 ml plain,
unsweetened yoghurt

5 fl oz/150 ml double cream

1. Pour the water and lemon juice into a saucepan; next add the sugar and heat the ingredients slowly, until all the sugar has melted.

2. Increase the heat until the syrup reaches boiling point.

3. Remove the saucepan from the heat and spoon a little of the syrup onto a saucer – about one tablespoon will do. If the syrup forms a skin, and you find it has a sticky consistency when you push it back lightly with your little finger, you will know that it is ready. If the syrup is slightly too watery, then let it simmer for another minute or two before carrying out the same test once more.

4. Add the marmalade to the syrup and mix well.

5. Mix the yoghurt and cream together well in a bowl. Next add the syrup and mix before pouring the mixture into an ice cream maker; leave for 20 minutes. If you do not have a machine, pour the mixture into an appropriate dish and place in the freezer. Stir with a fork every 30 minutes until it is set.

Chocolate Truffles

1. Break the chocolate into small pieces and place into a food processor until the chocolate forms small granules.

2. Pour the cream and rum (or brandy) into a saucepan and add the butter; heat until the mixture is simmering.

3. Switch the food processor on again – this time on a much slower speed – so that all the ingredients mix together until they are of a smooth consistency.

4. Add the yoghurt and mix the ingredients for a few extra seconds.

5. Leave the mixture to cool, then transfer to a bowl and cover with some clingfilm before placing in the fridge overnight.

6. The following day, you will see that the mixture has thickened. Ginger, almonds or plain cocoa powder may be added to the truffle mixture to create a tasty variety.

5 oz/150 g good quality plain chocolate

5 fl oz/150 ml thick double cream

1 oz/25 g unsalted butter

2 tbsp rum or brandy

1 tbsp Greek yoghurt

Brazil Nuts with Butter Toffee

3 oz/75 g unsalted butter
8 oz/225 g dark soft brown sugar
8 oz/225 g Brazil nuts

1. Melt the butter in a saucepan. Add the sugar and mix together well over a low heat until it becomes dark brown in colour.

2. Add the nuts, a few at a time, and mix until they are covered with the toffee.

3. Use some butter to grease a plate, then lift the toffee-coated nuts from the saucepan (using a draining spoon).

4. When the toffee has cooled and hardened over the nuts, transfer the sweets into small paper cases.

You can also use the following fruits instead of the nuts: tangerine segments, grapes, figs or strawberries. Use a cocktail stick to dip the fruits in the toffee mixture.

FOR MORE COOKBOOKS, Welsh language tutors, books about Welsh art, music and politics… greetings cards, diaries, t-shirts and much more – send now for your free copy of our full-colour 48-page catalogue…

…or simply surf into our interactive web-site!

Talybont
Ceredigion
SY24 5AP
Cymru/Wales

tel +44 (0)1970 832 304 **fax** 832 782 **isdn** 832 813
e-mail ylolfa@ylolfa.com **www** www.ylolfa.com